© Copyright by Bim Bam Bom Funny Joke Books. Images Feepik.com or licensed for commercial use. All rights reserved.

Q: How many rappers will it take to change a lightbulb?
A: None. They are all too lil' to reach it.

I've been reading a book about anti-gravity until 3 am. It's impossible to put down!

I would like to go on a diet, but I just have way too much on my plate right now.

Q: What do you call a dog magician?
A: A labracadabrador!

Q: How did the eggs leave the highway?
A: They went through the eggs-it.

My wife accused me of being childish. I told her to get out of my tipi!

The nurse just informed me that the doctor can no longer perform the transplant. The surgeon wanted to tell me himself, but he didn't have the heart.

I like telling dad jokes. Sometimes he laughs!

Q: What did baby corn say to mommy corn?
A: Where's popcorn?

Q: What kind of books do bunnies read?
A: The ones with hoppy endings!

I came up with this hilarious joke about construction. I'm still working on it, though...

Q: Why are skeletons never stressed?
A: Because nothing gets under their skin.

Q: Why do some couples get a membership at the gym?
A: Because they want their relationship to work out!

Q: How do you get a farm girl's attention?
A: A tractor!

Q: How does a penguin build its house?
A: Igloos it together!

Q: What did the fisherman say to the magician?
A: Pick a cod, any cod!

Q: The drummer had twin daughters, What did he call them?
A: Anna one, Anna two!

Did you hear about the new restaurant that opened up downtown, called Karma? They don't have a menu. You simply get what you deserve!

Q: If a plane crashed on the border of the U.S. and Mexico, in which country would the survivors be buried?
A: Nowhere, you don't bury survivors!

Q: How do you get a squirrel to like you?
A: Act like a nut.

I'm an expert at sleeping. I'm so good at it, I can do it with my eyes closed!

Q: Why does the ghost always need more books?
A: He goes through them too quickly.

Q: Why was the math book sad?
A: Because it had so many problems.

Q: What do you call the wife of a hippie?
A: Mississippi.

Q: How does one lawyer say goodbye to the other?
A: I'll be suing ya!

Q: How do little bees travel to school?
A: They take the school buzz!

Q: What is orange and really bad for your teeth?
A: A brick.

Q: What did one hat say to the other hat?
A: Stay here, I'll go on a head.

Q: How do baby chickens dance?
A: Chick-to-chick!

Q: What do you get if you cross a cocker spaniel, a poodle and a rooster?
A: Cockerpoodledoo!

Two dads are sitting on opposite sides of a river. One dad yells to the other: "How do I get to the other side of the river?" The other dad replies: "You ARE on the other side!"

Q: What did the little candle say to the big candle?
A: I'm going out tonight!

My wife is really annoyed at the fact that I don't have any sense of direction. So I packed my things and right.

I imagined there'd be more training when I became a garbageman, but you really just pick it up as you go.

Q: What do you call a fake noodle?
A: Impasta!

My friend tried to cheer me up when I was feeling down. He said "Come on man, things could have been much worse. You could have been stuck underground in a hole full of water!" I know he means well.

Two goldfish are in a tank when one says to the other, "Do you know how to drive this thing?"

The Soviet Union was never gonna work, it had to fail. The red flags were everywhere.

Q: Why did the photograph have to go to jail?
A: Because it was framed.

Q: Where do lizards go when their tails fall off?
A: The re-tail store!

Q: What do you call a cat that lives in an igloo?
A: An eskimeow!

Q: What do you call a man who can't stand?
A: Neil

A King, who's is very fond of animals and has his own zoo, hosts a Royal Dinner Party for all the important people in the country. To impress his guests, he has asked his staff to put some of his most-loved animals in the party room. One of the animals in the room, a penguin, lets out a loud fart. The King turns to him and says: "How dare you fart in front of me!" The penguin replies: "I'm terribly sorry, your Highness, I didn't realize it was your turn!"

To the man in the wheelchair that stole my camouflage pants...You can hide but you can't run.

Q: How does Jennifer Lopez stay cool?
A: She has many fans!

Q: Why did the coffee go to the police station and file a report?
A: Because it got mugged.

If two vegans argue and get into a fight, is it still considered a beef?

Q: What will the Terminator be called after he retires?
A: The Exterminator!

Frank: "Did you hear the news about the kidnapping at school?" John: "Yes, I saw it. You don't need to worry about it though. He just woke up."

Q: What is a cat's favorite dessert?
A: Mice Cream!

If you ever want to know how to build an ark, let me know. I Noah guy!

I wanted to lose weight, so I briefly considered going on an all-almond diet. But I realized that was just nuts.

Q: Which bear is the most condescending?
A: A pan-duh!

Q: How do monsters like their eggs?
A: Terri-fried!

A polar bear walks into a job center. "Wow, a talking polar bear," says the clerk. "With your talent, we will definitely be able to find you a job in the circus." "The circus?" says the polar bear, disappointed: "Why would a circus want to hire an electrician?"

Did I tell you about the restaurant on the moon? Excellent steak, but no atmosphere.

Q: What do you call a pig that practices karate?
A: A pork chop!

Q: What has two butts and kills people?
A: An assassin!

Q: It has has been lying at the bottom of the ocean for centuries and twitches. What is it?
A: A nervous wreck.

Q: What is orange and sounds like a parrot?
A: A carrot!

Q: What's an astronaut's favorite key on a computer keyboard?
A: The space bar!

A woman is on trial for hitting her husband with his guitars. In court, the Judge asks, "First offender?" "No," she replies, "First a Gibson, then a Fender!"

Q: What did the pirate say on his 80th birthday?
A: Aye matey!

A cheese sandwich walks into a bar and orders a drink. The bartender says, "I'm sorry, but we don't serve food here."

Q: Why did all the students in class eat their homework?
A: Because their teacher told them: "It's a piece of cake!"

Did you hear about the koala who invented the knock knock joke? He won the no-bell prize!

Q: Where are chicks born?
A: In Chick-cago.

Q: How many burritos can you eat on an empty stomach?
A: Just one, because then your stomach won't be empty.

Some folks say they pick their nose, but I was just born with mine.

Q: What do you call an elephant that doesn't matter?
A: An irrelephant.

Q: What do you call a dog who designs buildings?
A: A bark-itect.

Q: Why shouldn't you tell an egg a joke?
A: Because it might crack up!

A chicken was going to America. After she left, her best friend was asked where she was going. She said "I don't know, but definitely not to Kentucky!"

Q: How does a snowman go to work?
A: He takes his icicle!

A termite walks into a bar and asks, "Is the bar tender here?"

Q: What do you call someone without a body and nose?
   A: Nobody knows!

If a child refuses to go to sleep at night, is it guilty of resisting a rest?

Q: What is the least spoken language in the world?
A: Sign language!

My daughter asked me, "Dad, what was your favorite band growing up?" "Led Zeppelin," I replied. She said: "Who?" "Yes," I said, "They were good, too."

Q: What would you say is the best part about living in Switzerland?
A: I don't know, but the flag is a big plus!

Q: What do you call a bear with no teeth?
A: A gummy bear!

Can February March? No, but April May!

When a woman is giving birth, she is literally kidding.

Q: Why did the lobster not share his food?
A: Because he's shellfish!

Q: Which dinosaur knows the most synonyms?
A: Thesaurus!

Q: Why was the scarecrow awarded a prize?
A: Because he was outstanding in his field.

It takes guts to be an organ donor...

I don't really like to go to funerals that start before midday. I guess I'm just not a mourning person!

Q: What is a dog's favorite kind of pizza?
A: Pupperoni!

Q: What does a computer eat when it's hungry?
A: Microchips!

Q: What did the grape do when someone stepped on it?
A: He let out a little wine.

Q: What kind of music do elves like?
A: "Wrap" music!

Q: What was Beethoven's favorite fruit?
Q: Ba-na-na-na!

Q: Which side of a chicken has more feathers?
A: The outside.

Q: Can a kangaroo jump higher than the Statue of Liberty?
A: Of course! The Statue of Liberty can't jump, silly.

Q: Why did the pirate not know the alphabet?
A: He always gets stuck at 'C'!

Q: What is the cat's favorite movie?
A: The Sound of Meowsic.

Q: When does a joke turn into a dad joke?
A: When it becomes apparent....

Q: A boy volcano was located close to a girl volcano. What did he say to her?
A: "I lava you..."

Q: If you have 15 oranges in one hand and 12 bananas in the other, what do you have?
A: Big hands!

Q: What type of nails do carpenters not like to hit?
A: Fingernails!

Q: Who can drink a gallon of gasoline without dying?
A: Jerry can!

Q: What did the buffalo say to his son when he dropped him off at school?
A: Bison.

A man tried to start a fight with me by throwing Mozzarella cheese, dough, and tomato sauce at me. So I yelled at him, "Do you wanna pizza me?"

Did you hear the rumor about butter? Well, I'm not a gossiper, so I'm not going to spread it...

Yesterday, I was arrested for stealing cooking utensils from the store. No regrets though, it was worth the whisk.

Q: What do marathon runners eat before the race starts?
A: Nothing, they fast!

I'm going to see the doctor tomorrow to ask him to remove my spine. I feel like it's just holding me back.

Q: Why is Peter Pan always flying in the air?
A: Because he neverlands!

I know a handful of funny jokes about retired people but none of them work!

A beaver's tail makes it look odd. But without it, it would look even otter.

Q: What are your thoughts on glass coffins, will they become popular?
A: Well, that remains to be seen.

Q: How does a lion greet the other animals in the field?
A: "Pleased to eat you!"

Q: What kind of horse eats with their ears?
A: They all do! Who removes their ears before dinner?

Q: What do you call a man with a rubber toe?
A: Roberto!

Did you hear about the Italian cook who died recently? He pasta way!

Q: What sound does the car of a witch make?
A: Broom Broom!

Q: What did the cat say when it was on the phone?
A: "Can you hear meow?"

Q: What do you call a scary chicken?
A: A poultrygeist.

Q: What did the dolphin say when it bumped into the wall?
A: Dam!

Q: What did the prisoner use to call another prisoner?
A: A cell phone!

Q: Why are elevator jokes so good?
A: Because they work on many levels!

Q: What did the queen bee say to the lazy working bee?
A: Beehive yourself!

Q: Why did the chicken cross the ocean?
A: To get to the other tide.

Finally, spring is here. I got so excited this morning I wet my plants!

Did you hear? A cheese factory exploded in the south of France. The brie is everywhere!

Q: What did one wall say to the other wall?
A: "I will see you at the corner!"

Q: Which state has more streets than any other?
A: Rhode Island!

I sold my vacuum cleaner last week. It was just gathering dust!

The waitress walked up to the table and said: "I'm sorry about your wait." Dad replied, "Are you saying I'm fat?"

Q: Which state in the U.S. is well-known for its extra-small soft drinks?
A: Minnesota!

Four out of three people admit they're not good with fractions!

I would think twice before ordering sushi at this restaurant. It's a little fishy!

Q: How many pears grow on a tree?
A: All of them!

Q: Why are spiders so intelligent?
A: Because they can find everything on the web!

Many years ago, I had a job in a shoe-recycling shop. It was sole destroying!

Q: How are a dog and a marine biologist alike?
A: One wags a tail and the other tags a whale.

Months ago, I had a neck brace fitted. I've never looked back since!

Q: Why did the chicken go up the stairs?
A: She was already across the street.

Q: Why are trees so suspicious on sunny days?
A: Because they're a little shady!

Q: What happens when you visit the bathroom in Spain?
A: European.

Q: What do you call a bull that is sound asleep?
A: Bulldozer!

Q: Why did the old lady fall into the well?
A: Because she couldn't see that well!

Q: Why do melons get married?
A: Because they cantaloupe!

Q: What do you call a factory that sells passable products?
A: A satisfactory!

I don't play soccer because I enjoy the sport. I'm simply doing it for kicks!

Q: Why is it a bad idea to write a letter with a broken pencil?
A: Because it is pointless!

Q: What happens to the car of a frog when it breaks down?
A: The car gets toad away.

I told my daughter I was named after George Washington..."But dad," she said, "your name is Hank." "I know," I replied, "but I was named AFTER George Washington."

Q: What did the Atlantic ocean say to the Pacific ocean?
A: Nothing, they just waved.

Q: What do you call the security men keeping guard outside a Samsung shop?
A: Guardians of the Galaxy!

Q: How does a chicken tell time?
A: One o'cluck, two o'cluck, three o'cluck...

Q: What is the favorite meal of a whale?
A: A peanut butter and jellyfish sandwich!

Q: What did the banana say, when he walked into the doctor's office?
A: "Doctor, I am not peeling well."

Q: What do you call an insect that bites you during a service?
A: A Mosque-ito!

Q: What do chickens study in school?
A: Eggonomics.

Q: What did the cop say to his belly button?
A: You are under a vest!

Q: What does a chicken have in common with a band?
A: Drumsticks

I wrote a book on flamingos. In hindsight, paper would probably have been easier...

I don't understand why people say that age is just a number. Age is clearly a word.

Are you ready for a joke about a piece of paper? Never mind... it's tearable.

Q: Why does a seagull fly over the sea?
A: Because if it flew over the bay, it would be called a bagull!

Q: What would you get if you crossed a giraffe with an ant?
A: A giant!

Q: What do you call a dog with a surround system?
A: A sub-woofer!

Q: How do you get a tissue to dance?
A: You put a little boogie in it!

Q: Two toilet rolls are sitting in a bar. What did the first toilet roll say to the other?
A: "People keep on ripping me off!"

Q: What is even more amazing than a talking bear?
A: A spelling bee

Q: Why did the ants dance on top of the jam jar?
A: The lid read: 'Twist to open'!

Q: What are a ninja's favorite kind of shoes?
A: Sneakers.

Q: What do you call cheese that isn't yours?
A: Nacho cheese!

Q: If you were to cross a dog and a calculator, what would you get?
A: A friend you can count on!

Q: At what time did the man have his dentist appointment?
A: Tooth hurt-y!

Q: What did the left eye say to the right eye?
A: Between you and me, there is something that smells.

The doctor just diagnosed me as color blind. It really came out of the yellow.

Why did the invisible man turn down the job offer? He couldn't see himself doing it...

Q: What does a super angry pepper do?
A: It gets jalapeño face...

Q: How many tickles does it take to make an octopus laugh?
A: Ten tickles!

Q: Why can't a nose be 12 inches long?
A: Because then it would be a foot!